David,

I loved meeting you.

Best wishes with your
move and much success
in your life.

To your rePURPOSED Mind,

Joshua

re PURPOSE
your
MIND

re PURPOSE
your
MIND

**Lessons to move from
a stuck mindset to consistent,
PURPOSE driven success**

JOSHUA DAHLSTROM

ISBN: 978-1-64999-460-8

Published by Abundance Books, LLC
601 E Sherman Ave Ste 5
Coeur d'Alene, ID 83814

ABUNDANCE

DEDICATION

This book is dedicated to my kids. Meshach,
Xanaia, Kydan, and Brax; may you dream big and find
happiness in pursuit of your Vision.

CONTENTS

rePURPOSE your MIND

INTRODUCTION

DISCOVERING YOUR PURPOSE

There was once a time, when you believed absolutely anything was possible. At that time, the world was open to you. You had freedom in your life and you felt like you could conquer the world. Over time you experienced heartbreak from friends who betrayed you, or unexpected challenges and disappointments along the way, or perhaps illness and death of loved ones. You began to see the limitations of dollars because they only went so far, and the limitations of transportation because you only had so much time. Travelling lost some excitement when you realized wherever you went cost money. You felt the world closing in on you with each new realization.

The purpose of this book is to wake up that person inside of you who still believes anything is possible, to open your heart and mind to all the possibilities you once believed.

It is easy to look back on these prior beliefs with longing. Thinking, if I could go back to myself before I ventured down this current path, I would tell myself to

'Do what you love. Don't ever allow other people's expectations to limit your personal beliefs."

So, instead of just thinking, speak to that person inside you who still believes. Say it out loud. Wake up to what you really wanted in life. Stop using the years of excuses, time, money, or lack of support as excuses for not doing what you love. Break down those barriers and discover what's possible. Ask yourself, "What can I do, and what am I willing to do? Where will my passion lead me?" Your answers to these questions will help you make a list that you can use to guide you to fulfilling your passion. Once you've got the list, just do it. Mark that first thing off your list. Then keep checking off one box at a time, until you are on your way.

This book is not here to make you feel good, though it will lift you up. This book is not another quick-read you will leave on the shelf as you return to your normal life...

This book is for people who not only want, but are willing to, *change*.

Without action, change is simply a word. When you are willing to take actionable steps to change, you will know your passion and reach your vision. Your vision is your inspiration on this journey.

You take your first actionable step when you rePURPOSE your Mind and return to the self who believed anything was possible. When you rePURPOSE your Mind to that state, you switch your mind from cautious and closed, to open and ambitious. Ask your adolescent self, "If you were in charge of my business, relationship, or life, how would you handle it today?"

If you truly immerse yourself in this book, and rePURPOSE your Mind, one chapter at a time, you will experience something similar to binge watching a series on Netflix. At first, you simply like the series, and then before you know it, you love watching it every chance you get. Then, when it's over, you think, "What do I do now?" You don't just binge watch the series and then slip back into your life, spending those hours the way you used to. You find another show to fill that void. Before you know it, you have dedicated endless hours to binge watching TV. You might not even remember what you did with those hours before Netflix binging entered your life.

The same phenomenon will unfold if you immerse yourself in this book, applying the concepts to your life one day at a time. Like a Netflix binge, you will like it at first, and then you will fall into a pattern you love. You will begin to see how rePURPOSING your Mind changes how you act, think and live. This shift however, isn't a passive Netflix Binge, it requires time, practice, and of course, action. Completing this book, finding a coach, and continuing to receive support from a wingman will launch you on the path to your inspired vision and purpose. We're always here for you at rePURPOSEDMIND.com to support you on your journey.

This book is here to help you find your passion that will lead you to your purpose. Not someone else's, YOURS! When you find YOUR purpose you no longer worry about what others think of you, what they are doing, or what they will say. Once you find your purpose, discovering your path in life and the steps along the way become clear.

I'm going to tell you a story about the steps I took after discovering I needed to make a change in my life. This story is about not giving up. It's also about realizing I needed to take action and needed help to make that happen. I reached out to an unlikely wingman for that help.

DISCOVERING MY PURPOSE

As a teen, I was very reckless and got involved in many things that were bad for me: drugs, alcohol, parties, etc. One day, I woke up and looked at all the guys lying around my house after a party the night before. I thought, "What a bunch of losers!" The thought barely entered my mind when I realized, "I'm a loser too!" I was about a third of the way to sleeping on someone else's floor, just like these guys were sleeping on mine.

Then I heard, "You deserve more. You are a child of God." That is when I decided I was going to be more. At that moment, I began to shift my thoughts. I began to understand my greater value to God, to myself, and to those around me.

Anyone who has lived that lifestyle knows it's not easy to let go of it. There are temptations everywhere. You might be surrounded by people who pressure you to keep using, to take another hit, drink, or bump. In order to truly move forward, you have to cut all ties and maybe even continue alone, until you discover people who support you in making a change in your life. Needless to say, it's not always easy to move forward alone.

On my journey, I felt incredibly alone, as if every step was met with resistance. I was sure my efforts toward change would be suffocated by that loneliness. So, that's when I turned to God. I prayed, "Give me someone to come back to you with, and I will turn away from my past and toward you 100%."

God didn't waste any time.

Soon after that prayer, I stopped by a local gas station to flirt with the cashier. She wasn't working that day so I decided to go to a different gas station with better snacks. As I walked in, I looked to my left and there stood an angel behind the counter. I fell in love the moment I saw her.

Yes, it was love at first sight.

I grabbed my snacks and headed to the checkout, but there was a problem. Two women were working, and the woman who caught my eye was very popular. Everyone seemed to gravitate toward her line. I knew I couldn't just stand in her line when there was another register open so I kept myself busy. The shelves by her register had PowerBars. I didn't like PowerBars. I feigned a great love for them in that moment. The minute her register was open, I grabbed a PowerBar and approached her. I was so nervous I could not think of anything to say other than lame pickup lines from years of hitting on girls at parties. So, I smiled and walked away, with a PowerBar I'd never eat and maybe even an answer from God.

I needed to meet this girl.

I continued to visit her gas station for quite some time. I often filled up my gas tank long before the needle had ticked past the ¾ mark. Yet still, even with the frequent visits, my words came out scrambled and shy as I handed her my credit card for $10 fill-ups.

One day, I decided I couldn't keep dragging my feet, I was going to ask this girl out. I needed a little courage, so I asked God for some help. In that moment, he sent me another unlikely wingman. There was a man on the side of the freeway with his thumb out. I picked up the hitchhiker and told him, "You're gonna help me get a date today."

He responded, "Whatever, as long as you buy me some cigarettes."

I rambled on about her for an hour as we drove. Somehow, recounting everything I loved about this girl already, gave me the confidence to finally ask her out. I entered the store, grabbed my pizza and apple juice, looked once again at the PowerBars, checked out, and then almost walked away. At the last moment, I heard myself say, "So, are you the kind of girl that would go out with a guy like me?"

WHAT!? I couldn't believe what I had just said. I wanted to shove those words far back down my throat where they came from.

I was mortified!

I couldn't believe that after three weeks of building up the courage to ask her out, that was my pickup line. I wanted to put those words back into my mouth.

She grabbed my hand and pulled it toward her, inspecting the ring I was wearing that symbolized my belief in Christ as my Savior.

Then she said, "Yes, I think I am!"

I wore that ring every day, even during my rough years, to remind me what I believed in. That ring had kept me from toppling over the edge, down a path I couldn't come back from. It anchored me. The moment this girl grabbed my hand, zeroed in on the ring, and said yes, I felt as if I'd betrayed her. In that moment, she didn't know who I had been, she only saw who I wanted to become.

None of that mattered though. She had said YES! So, we set the date for Thursday. It was only a couple days away.

Elated, I told the hitchhiker, "She said yes!"

He asked me, "So what's her name?"

Uh, I didn't know. I went back into the store to awkwardly ask her. Her name was Bridgette.

When I got back to the car, the hitchhiker said, "Tell me you got her number." No, I had not gotten her number. So, once again, I climbed back out of the car and shuffled back into the store to get her number. The hitchhiker thought I was crazy.

As we drove down the road, I suddenly remembered that I was going to be out of town on Thursday. So, I turned around and went back AGAIN, this time to change the date. When I told her I needed to reschedule, her face fell but she reluctantly agreed.

When the day of our date finally arrived, I gave her a call. I had been really busy and hadn't made it back to her store to check in with her since we'd set the date.

There was no one answer.

"Nothing to worry about," I thought, "Just give it a few minutes and I'm sure she'll answer." I waited five minutes and called again. No answer. I waited ten minutes and called again. No answer.

As those 10 minutes ticked by, I felt myself getting upset, so when I called back again, I left a hasty message on her answering machine, assuming she had blown me off.

It's never a good idea to assume, because I had no idea that the night before, her brother got caught talking to his girlfriend on the phone at 2 AM. Her mom had taken all the phones with her shopping. So, when I left that message on her answering machine, Bridgette was able to listen but had no way to respond.

I sat there, beating myself up because I was sure Bridgette had been God's answer to my prayer. On the other hand, I thought I was kind of crazy for believing it could happen so fast. As my doubts began to creep in, I decided to forget about Bridgette. I would go have some fun on my own instead.

I stopped by the gas station to grab a snack, knowing Bridgette wouldn't be working since we were *supposed to be* on a date. I grabbed my pizza and apple juice and stood in front of a cashier. Suddenly a frantic woman ran in. It was Bridgette. She jumped behind the counter, picked up the phone, and dialed.

My cell phone rang.

Surprised, she turned around and said, "I'm really sorry." She told me about her brother and her mom, and I sighed with relief. Maybe this was God's answer after all. I risked it and asked, "So how about that date?"

There was no time for dinner before the activity I planned for the date, so I suggested we grab another pizza and apple juice and hit the road. She asked if I was going to grab a PowerBar, I smiled sheepishly and shook my head no (I already had the girl, I didn't need the PowerBar).

We went out to the car and I opened her door for her. As I walked back around the car to get in, I watched her lean her arm against the center console and she seemed to tip her head to the side in confusion when the console refused to close. Curious, she peeked inside and found a mountain of PowerBars. When I got in the car, she turned to me, "There are a lot of PowerBars in there; don't you eat those?" Without thinking, I responded, "No I don't even like them. Help yourself."

We spent the evening playing disc golf and had an amazing time. I realized I really liked this girl, but felt guilty, as if she didn't know the real me. Midway through our date, I told her how much I liked her and quickly admitted, "But I need to be honest with you. When I asked you out on this date, you grabbed my hand, and when you saw my ring you said yes. I need you to know, that's not me. It's not who I am, or who I have been. It's just a reminder of who I want to be. I don't want you to date me because of my ring. That wouldn't be fair."

She looked at me and she said, "That's ok. You've got potential." God had indeed answered my prayer and in turn strengthened my belief in myself. Bridgette also believed in me and she eventually said yes to be my companion for the rest of our lives.

I shared this story with you because it became my turning point. This book began in that moment. God answered my prayer and sent me an angel to help me realize my full purpose.

Every person's turning point begins with a realization that there is a greater purpose.

When you discover your purpose, you have the opportunity to rePURPOSE your Mind. With a rePURPOSED MIND, you can follow your purpose to success. Once you know your purpose you *will* achieve success. You *will* rediscover the passion that inspires the person inside you who believes you can do anything.

Undeniably, it helps to find a wingman. Bridgette became my first wingman. As I have continued my journey in my own purpose, I have found incredible people to provide the right support and coaching.

You don't have to walk your path alone. As you read through this book, think about how you can call in the right wingman for you as you repurpose you're Mind and create the life you envision through the lessons in this book.

Will your wingman be a spiritual guide? Maybe yours will be a close friend, a spouse, or a business mentor. Perhaps you'll find your greatest success if your wingman is a coach.

START WITH WHO

When you think about who you want to become, what version of "you" inspires excitement? Sparks your ambition? Moves you so deeply you *find it difficult* to stop yourself from jumping in with both feet to become the best version of "you" *right now*?

Close your eyes and imagine making this "you" a reality. Think about the passion you feel as that person. Envision who you will be, what you will do, and how you will achieve success as this person. Grab that vision and hold on tight!

Write down that vision right now. Use the margins of this book. Grab a piece of paper or a notebook. Write it down in this moment or it could escape. Go ahead, I'll wait for you. Taking this action right now will show that you are committed.

To achieve your vision, you must have a strong *desire* to sustain your journey. You must also have a lot of motivation and commitment. So, the question is, where can you find a strong enough power source to propel you from who you are now, to who you want to be?

The answer starts with *Who*.

Who can you see yourself becoming after you complete the necessary work? The choice is yours, and the opportunities are as abundant as your willingness to act upon them.

Author Simon Sinek famously encourages his readers to "Start with Why". In his widely viewed 2009 TED Talk, Sinek explains this message, "People don't buy what you do. They buy *why* you do it." When you really get down to it, many products and services aren't particularly unique. As a result, it can be tough to sell your products if their value is based solely on their inherent features. Sinek claims the "solution" is simply to recognize where people's passions lie. Your product itself doesn't motivate buyers to hand over their hard-earned money. Instead, your reason *why* motivates your buyers to do so. It's not your product that moves people, but your *purpose*. And where does your purpose originate? You guessed it, with *who you are*. So, **start with *Who*.**

While Sinek primarily focuses on corporate marketing, by adding some creative thinking, you can apply his idea to discovering your passion, and then achieving your own purpose and highest version of self. While Sinek encourages his audience to start with their "Why," I'm inviting you to start with your *Who*. Who are you going to become?

The possibilities are as limitless as your imagination. Do you dream of becoming a powerful tycoon who revolutionized an industry? A savvy entrepreneur creating a legacy of innovation? An investor with plenty of leisure time to devote to civic involvement? A devoted parent who never misses a school play, musical performance, or baseball game?

Whoever you envision yourself becoming, you'll need plenty of energy to get there. Your source for that energy is a clear vision for your future self. This vision will provide a well-spring of commitment and motivation when you're feeling low on energy and willpower.

The journey of a thousand successes begins with the first step. So, start your journey with *Who*.

LESSON

To be able to rePURPOSE your Mind to your success, you need to first clearly identify who you want to be.

TAKE ACTION

Create a repurpose Statement clearly identifying who you want to be - This is taking everything that you know, everything that you have experienced, and rePURPOSING it to success. You know who you want to be because you wrote it down earlier in this chapter. Add "who do you serve?" to that and you'll begin to see your rePURPOSE statement coming together.

This first step is so important. You should not turn the page until you have it written down. Your rePURPOSE

Statement will change as you change and that's ok. It will evolve as you become who you want to be.

SAMPLE STATEMENTS

Need help? Follow this pattern from earlier in the chapter: "Who you will be, what you will do, and how you will achieve success." Add "who you serve."

"I will be an artist that creates fun ways to express myself while teaching others to enjoy art too. I will serve people by providing classes on how to draw."

"I am becoming a teacher for people who want to learn to code. My focus is parents who want to code with their kids."

"I am going to be someone who is fun to be around. I will learn how to skydive and scuba dive this year with at least one friend."

Your rePURPOSE Statement:

_____

_____

_____

_____

DEFINE YOUR SUCCESS

When you meet someone for the first time, after you ask their name, what question do you follow up with? Most people ask, "What do you do?" It's a simple question. You ask this question to learn who someone is and what their passion in life is. It helps you understand what the other person values.

This is a problem.

Why? Not everyone chooses a career path based on their values. Who you are is not defined by what you do. Instead, what you do *should be* defined by who you are.

So, why is this important? When you choose to focus your energy on a certain path, based on anything other than YOUR passion, you find yourself chasing fulfillment and *success* but never achieving it.

Success is often defined as a flourishing business built from scratch. It is often a leader at the head of a top corporation or a person living a life full of wealth and abundance. Once again, this view of success is a problem when so broadly applied. This is only the path to success for someone who finds true value in this particular measurement.

Creating a business, climbing to the top of the ladder, and building abundant wealth are not the only paths to success. Success can also be found in your emotional well-being, relationships, hobbies, and in many other parts of your life.

For you, success might be found in achieving a certain position in your company or in making a specific amount of money. Success could even come from simply finding joy in the things you do, or having your own family. It may be found in overcoming addiction, or finding peace from a troubled past. Perhaps you'll even find it in traveling the world with your best friend. The options are endless; the definition of success for you will be built upon your values and passions.

Nobel Prize Winner, Albert Schweitzer, says, "Success is not the key to happiness. Happiness is the key to success. If you love what you are doing, you will be successful." He is telling us that we should rePURPOSE our Minds to focus on happiness and we will find the key to success.

Now that you have created your rePURPOSED Statement, you will begin seeing success by knowing that purpose and then continually pursuing it. Achieving success looks different for every individual because everyone has a different purpose. To create your version of success, you must first rePURPOSE your Mind to happiness. This will direct YOUR passion.

In his book, *The Achievement Habit*, Bernard Roth walks you through an exercise to help you identify your purpose, or endgame as he calls it. He begins with five simple questions you should ask yourself:

1. Imagine you have only ten minutes to live. What would you do?

2. Imagine you have only ten days to live. What would you do?

3. Imagine you have only ten months to live. What would you do?

4. Imagine you have only ten years to live. What would you do?

5. Imagine you have only the rest of your life to live. What would you do?

When you answer these questions, you begin to understand what your core values are. You learn what is really important in your life. You understand your passion. Roth goes on to ask, "Can you think of any changes you would like to design into your self-image? Start designing and changing! [No one knows when they will enter their final countdown.] I don't know when mine will come, and you don't know yours either. One thing for sure—it is closer today than it was yesterday, and it will be closer still tomorrow. So now is the time to develop into the person you want to be."

He goes on to encourage you to ask four other questions:

● "Who am I?"

● "What do I want?"

- "What is my purpose?"

- "What do I really want?"

Roth says you need to "keep asking it, over and over, until you feel you have gained insight into your own desires so you're no longer at the mercy of society's ideas of what is good for you."

I would have you ask a few more questions. What do you want your legacy to be? What really matters to you? If time and money were not factors, what would you like to do, be, or have? How can you best contribute to the world?

Answering these questions honestly will help you identify your core values. Identifying your values clarifies your purpose and inspires you to take action toward success.

Identifying *your* core values can sometimes be challenging. I was working through a Core Values exercise with one of my clients when she shared her frustration with identifying her personal core values. She had a list of three, but they seemed to shuffle themselves around depending whether she was at work, at home or by herself. She asked me, "How do I balance these values that come in conflict with each other?" Once we looked more closely, she realized they all represented the same core value: service. She learned that they were not in conflict with each other. That's when she rePURPOSED her Mind. She began to look at how to provide the best service in each situation based on the needs of those around her. She found that others responded in positive ways and she accomplished more in less time than she ever had before.

Allow your core values to be *yours*. For example, my core values are fun, family and service. As a religious man, I have wondered if my core values should have mentioned God. Honoring God is very important to me. I find I can honor Him best by having fun, focusing on my family, and serving others. For me, He is in all those things. I am ok if others view this differently than me because these values are my own, not theirs. Only you can define your core values.

When your core values support YOUR purpose, you are freed from other's expectations. You no longer worry about what people think or say, because you deeply understand what success looks like for you. Once you've stepped into your purpose, you are ready to take action toward achieving your vision. These actions will create positive results. You may even grow closer to your family and friends, or end up spending more time serving others. The choice is yours.

Remember, how you identify your success matters. Make it YOURS!

LESSON

When you choose to focus your energy on a certain path based on anything other than YOUR passion and purpose, you find yourself chasing fulfillment and success all your life, but you never achieve it. How you identify success matters. Your core values are the foundation.

TAKE ACTION

Review the answers you gave to the following questions:

What do you want your legacy to be?

What really matters to you?

If time and money were not factors, what would you like to do, be, or have?

How can you best contribute to the world?

Compare your answers to find similarities. What stands out to you? Out of all the answers that you wrote down, what are the top three things that speak to you? Let this happen naturally. Do not look for things that represent only who you are or only who you want to be. Look for what speaks to the values you represent.

In her book, dare to Lead, Brené Brown talks about the importance of knowing your values to help you become a leader. The following list includes suggestions from Brené's List of VALUES as well as some of my own. Use this list to help you identify your core values; circle those that jump out at you or write your own. Recognizing these will help guide you throughout your life.

Achievement	Adventure	Affirmation
Ambition	Authenticity	Balance
Being the best	Belonging	Career
Caring	Charity	Collaboration
Commitment	Community	Compassion
Competence	Confidence	Connection
Contribution	Cooperation	Courage

Creativity	Curiosity	Discipline
Diversity	Efficiency	Equality
Ethics	Excellence	Fairness
Faith	Family	Forgiveness
Freedom	Friendship	Fun
Generosity	Giving-gifts	Grace
Gratitude	Growth	Health
Honesty	Hope	Humility
Humor	Inclusion	Independence
Initiative	Intimacy	Integrity
Intuition	Joy	Justice
Kindness	Knowledge	Leadership
Learning	Leisure	Love
Loyalty	Nature	Openness
Optimism	Patience	Patriotism

Peace	Perseverance	Power
Recognition	Reliability	Resourcefulness
Respect	Responsibility	Risk taking
Safety	Security	Service
Simplicity	Spirituality	Sportsmanship
Success	Teamwork	Thrift
Travel	Trust	Truth
Understanding	Uniqueness	Vision
Vulnerability	Wealth	Wellbeing

Now that you have identified your core values, they will guide your purpose because they are key to what you will say yes or no to from now on. When you're able to say no to the things that aren't in line with your core values, you will actually have more time to know your purpose. Your purpose begins to become clearer. The things that are in line with your core values begin to define your purpose.

IT'S YOUR PURPOSE, OWN IT!

Taking ownership is an essential part of your unique journey. You discover your power when your ideas, purpose, actions and vision are driven by your passion. This creates a filter that every idea passes through while you decide if it is worth pursuing.

When making a decision, you may sometimes feel stuck because you apply someone else's filter to your own idea without realizing it. When someone asserts judgement over your idea, that person has stolen from you. Their judgement has applied their filter to your current and future ideas.

Every time you ponder your idea moving forward, you will likely question, "Would they like my idea? What would they think of my plan?" Soon enough, you may even feel the need to run all your ideas through their filter instead of your own.

So why is this a problem? When you apply someone else's filter instead of filtering your own ideas, your vision is no longer clear because you are always second-guessing the outcomes. Your ideas must run through your own filter because you are the person who is going to act upon them. You are the one who is responsible for bringing your ideas to fruition. You are the one who is either completely committed to your ideas, or only committed so long as someone else approves.

For example, I recently asked one of my coaching clients, "Why are you so stuck on this one idea?"

He said, "A friend who I really love and trust told me I needed to be worried about it."

I then asked, "How is placing worry on this one idea going to affect anything else that's going on?"

"I honestly don't know if it is," he replied.

After this interaction he assured me he was no longer worried, so we dropped it. About ten minutes later I circled back to make sure we'd found closure, and he said, "No, no, no! I don't want to spend my coaching time talking about something that doesn't really matter."

I stopped him and said, "I have circled back to your friend's judgement twice, because whether or not you see it, you continue to bring him up in our conservation. You also continue to shut me down and dismiss it when we try to unpack it."

After quietly thinking, he spoke, "I'm placing value in my friend's opinion when in reality I shouldn't be. What he thinks *really doesn't matter* when he is not the one doing the work, I am."

This time I could tell, he truly meant it. He had realized that running his ideas through his friend's filter, and making decisions based solely on another person's validation, was slowing him down. He was stalled because he couldn't act until someone else assured him it was okay to do so.

When you apply another person's filter over your unique idea, you create a problem for yourself. You not only give your idea away; you give your power away. Without your power to realize your own vision, you lose the ability to act strategically. You become stuck.

If you feel stuck, or if you've been chasing an idea for a while with no traction, ask yourself, "Why do I want to follow this idea? Why do I have this goal or dream?" If you happen to answer, "Because someone else said it was a good idea," you have applied someone else's filter to your purpose.

You may find yourself making choices and acting upon ideas because someone you love or respect recommends you do so. You might feel obligated to follow your loved one's advice because you don't want to disappoint or offend them. You may even think you should follow their advice simply because they are your friend, and you trust them.

When you choose to follow someone else's idea, you get stuck. You either don't have the motivation to follow this idea, or you flounder, not knowing how to proceed, because it wasn't your idea in the first place.

When you apply someone else's filter to your ideas, you are not being true to your own passion.

Knowing your core values gives you a purpose-driven filter to run your ideas through. This helps you ensure your ideas contribute to your purpose.

So, what is *your* purpose?

Often people think that their purpose should be based on things that everyone reaches for. A good example of this is, earning six figures, or locking down a job with a 401K... but is this really *your* purpose?

It's your purpose. Own it!

LESSON

Once you have identified YOUR purpose, it is then your responsibility to own it. When you allow someone else to influence your idea, you get stuck. It's your idea, it's your vision, it's your dream, it's your destination, all based on your passion and values, so own it.

TAKE ACTION

Using the core values that you identified in the previous chapter, find your Purpose by writing down the answers to each of these questions for each of your core values:

1. How am I going to have/give/be *Core Value*?

2. Who is going to benefit from *Core Value*?

3. How will I know when I have exemplified *Core Value*?

Now ask yourself, "Am I truly passionate about this purpose or am I doing it to please others?" This is most important. If you are doing it to please others, it is not *your* purpose it is theirs.

If you realize you do it to please others, you have made a breakthrough. You have learned how strong other people's filters can be.

Once you have done this exercise for all of your core values, combine the answers from question #3 for each value into a single purpose.

It is important to keep your focus on this Purpose.

Write your Purpose here. You will also want to put it somewhere you will see it often. Mine is written on my bathroom mirror where I can see it every day when I get up and every evening before going to bed.

You're Purpose:

_____

_____

_____

_____

_____

STAY FOCUSED ON YOUR PURPOSE

Any minister will tell you that simply discovering your purpose is a success.

"I found my calling in God, that's my purpose," they will say. Without doing anything, they will tell you, they are more successful than ever before. They have direction and they know what they need to do. They may be standing in front of a congregation or serving in a soup kitchen. It doesn't matter what their success looks like, as long as it's THEIR success.

Understanding your purpose is the key to understanding how to find YOUR success. Sometimes, when you become deeply entrenched in your path to success, you forget what your purpose is. Refocusing on what you want to achieve will remind you of what your purpose is.

Let me illustrate with the following story...

One day my kids were playing Monopoly and fighting about the rules.

I intervened, "What is your purpose in playing this game?"

They answered, "To win."

I responded, "That may be a secondary purpose, but what is the main reason you are playing with each other?"

They responded, "To have fun."

I asked, "Are you having fun?"

Looking down, they nodded their heads. "Yes," they lied.

"Ok, if everyone isn't following the same rules, can you all really have fun?"

They all agreed that no, they could not all have fun if they weren't on the same page about following the rules.

My kids allowed themselves to get distracted from their purpose when they became super focused on winning the game. When they all remembered that their true purpose was to have fun, they understood that by cheating they were not fulfilling their purpose. As a result, they were able to refocus on their purpose and find a way for everyone to have fun.

This is a simple illustration, but the same principle applies to you. When you find yourself feeling unsuccessful, you have likely strayed from your true purpose. I teach my clients five Rules of Purpose to help them stay focused and not get distracted by the process.

The Rules of Purpose

Understanding the Rules of Purpose will not only help you in times of disagreement with others, but it can help you recognize when you are in conflict with yourself. You will feel distracted and dissatisfied when you stray from your purpose.

The Rules of Purpose are adapted from the keynote speaker and corporate trainer, Galen Emanuele's "Rules of Improv." These rules are based on the "yes, and" mentality.

- Are you having fun?
- Are you staying positive?
- Do you embrace change and failure?
- Are you making others look good?
- Are you listening and being present?

I like to use a game Galen introduced to me to illustrate the Rules of Purpose: "Zip, Zap, and Zoom."

Let's begin with the *rules*. The *rules* of the game are the Rules of Purpose. However, the *directions* to this game are:

- zip goes right
- zap goes left
- and zoom goes anywhere you want

When I introduce this game to a group for the first time, we start zip. When "zap" is introduced, it doesn't take long for the participants to get confused and make mistakes. It is inevitable that someone will call out a person for "breaking the rules". At this point, I ask, "What are the rules of the game.

Generally, the person calling out the mistake, says, "Zip goes right, zap goes left."

I remind them that those are just the *directions*. The *rules* are the Five Rules of Purpose.

After this reminder, no one wants to call others out for their mistakes. However, the players making the mistakes begin to get frustrated with themselves. I stop the game here and say, "Hold on, don't forget to embrace change and failure, be positive and have fun. If you accept other people's mistakes, you must also accept your own."

This is often a place of realization. It's much harder to accept your own perceived failures than those of others. When you accept the Rules of Purpose in your own life, not just when playing games, but when working toward your goals, you have to remember they don't just apply to those you interact with, but they especially apply to yourself.

As "zoom" is introduced, players still get frustrated with keeping track of all the directions. I again stop the game and ask the question, "If zoom can go any direction, why are you still using zip and zap?"

My question in that moment is the same as my question to you now, "How many things are you holding onto because you think they are important, when in fact, they do not serve you?"

In life, "zoom" is your purpose. When you know your purpose, everything else is made easier or unnecessary.

Remember, purpose is a success the moment you discover it.

Once you know your purpose, there are no restrictions. Be positive, and have fun! If you aren't, step back and re-evaluate. Are you following the Five Rules of Purpose?

When you understand and stay focused on your purpose, it will lead you to your own unique success.

LESSON

Sometimes, when you get deeply entrenched in your path to success, you start to focus too much on the directions and not enough on the Five Rules of Purpose. If you find that you are not feeling successful, then you may not be meeting your purpose. As you adhere to the Five Rules of Purpose, you will be able to focus on the rules as you achieve success.

TAKE ACTION

Now that you know your Purpose, staying focused on it takes practice. Think about the times that you have succeeded in following your Purpose using the Rules of Purpose.

- When have you had fun?
- When were you positive?
- When did you embrace change or failure?

- When have you made others look good?

- When were you your best at being present and listening to someone else?

Now write it down, call a friend, and share it with the world. Celebrate this success. You didn't even know about the Rules of Purpose yet you succeeded in following them.

Now think about times when you could have followed the Rules of Purpose and how the outcome would have been different had you followed them. Think about how following the Rules of Purpose would have changed that experience. Learn from that experience! See how following the Rules of Purpose would change that moment and how it will change your future.

Now think forward. What interaction will you have tomorrow where you could intentionally practice the Rules of Purpose? Allow yourself to envision the entire experience following the Rules of Purpose. Practice it in your mind. Pick a time when you will do this every day for the next week.

As you practice the Rules of Purpose, you will begin to realize how much they open your life to so many possibilities. For years you "zipped" or "zapped" toward your goals, but now you know how to "zoom" forward and with that "zoom" you can go ANYWHERE and do ANYTHING.

USE THE FIVE PILLARS OF SUCCESS

Do you find your mind bursting with ideas of epic adventures you would like to experience, but never seem to follow through?

I have.

I learned long ago that if I am going to follow through on my *epic* ideas, I needed some way to sort through all of my ideas so that I could focus on those that were most promising and discard the ones that were not.

I use The Five Pillars of Success as a filter. I have been using this filter for years and have enjoyed some grand adventures. I have kayaked in the winter with Eagles flying overhead, swooping beside my kayak to pick up a Kokanee salmon. I've built snow caves with a scout troop of teenage boys and slept in it. I hiked to see a B-23 bomber crash site. I even presented on a TEDx stage in January 2020, teaching others how to turn their ordinary ideas into epic adventures by repurposing my Five Pillars of Success.

It was epic! You should check it out on YouTube.

These Five Pillars of Success have helped guide many people to finding their success. These Five Pillars are:

1. *Idea:* Every success starts with an idea. I don't believe there are good ideas or bad ideas, just ideas with high or low desire.

2. *Desire*: Is your desire high or low?

3. *Vision:* Vision is the cornerstone of everything else. You need to clearly visualize the end result.

4. *Motivation and Commitment:* Motivation is your why and this inspires Commitment. If your desire is high and your vision is clear then your commitment to stay the course remains strong.

5. *Willing Action:* To succeed, you must act. What are you willing to do to see your idea through to completion?

All of these point to and support your Vision, and your Vision is a product of your Purpose. Let me explain how each pillar works together.

IDEA

Every success starts with an idea. Too often, people quickly dismiss their own ideas because someone told them their idea wasn't good, or they choose to pursue an idea that someone else told them they should pursue.

If you try to pursue an idea through someone else's filter, you find your desire, commitment and motivation low. I discuss other people's filter in more depth later in this book. For now, remember to keep your ideas clear of other people's influence.

DESIRE

When you have an idea, measure it by your desire. How badly do you want to pursue this idea? Sometimes it helps to measure your desire on a scale of one to ten. If your desire is high, it is worth pursuing and if it's low, it's easy to eliminate. As you measure each idea by your desire, focus on those ideas where your desire is high.

For example, you may have an idea to buy a boat and sail the world, but your desire to actually do it may be a three. So you set the idea aside. You may also desire to pay off your house and you realize your desire for that is at an eight. When your desire is high, you willingly put your idea into action and take the steps necessary to succeed. Both of these options could take the same amount of effort and financial sacrifice, it is the measure of your desire that determines which idea to pursue.

VISION

Your vision is the cornerstone of everything else; it's the peak of the pyramid. What do you expect to get out of this? You must visualize how it will turn out and what that success looks like. You *must* have a clear vision in order to follow through to success.

MOTIVATION AND COMMITMENT

Your Motivation inspires your Commitment.

When thinking about your motivation, ask yourself why. Why do you want to achieve this vision? Do you seek notoriety and acclaim? Do you want to do it so your kids can have a better life than you had? Do you want to make the world a better place?

What is your WHY?

When everything starts to fall apart, how committed will you really be? If your desire is high and your vision is clear, your why will provide the motivation you need to keep your commitment strong.

WILLING ACTION

To succeed, you must take willing action. You must have purposeful movement toward your vision. What are you willing to do to make your Why happen?

If you have an idea, your desire is high, you can see a clear outcome, and your motivation and commitment are high, taking action should come naturally. With a high desire and commitment, fueled by your motivation, you will even desire to take action on tasks you may otherwise avoid. With each action you take, you come closer to making your vision a reality.

In all this your Vision is the key!

What is it you want? What does success in your Purpose look like to you? You MUST be able to see your Vision clearly because when you hit a roadblock and feel things begin to fall apart, it is your Vision that you go back to!

There will always be times that only you see your Vision. When things get tough, you take a deep breath and revisit that third pillar. You walk through The Five Pillars of Success with your eye on your Vision. What did you expect? Have you drifted away from your Vision? Did your Vision change? Is your commitment or desire not as strong as you thought they were? You analyze your actions. Are you blaming someone else for your inability to complete an action? Did you do what you said you would do? If not, you discover why. Then you redirect, recommit, or find a new path that will still lead to your Vision.

All of this starts with a clear Vision.

LESSON

Seeing your Vision clearly is the key to being able to follow your Purpose to Success. When your Vision is clear, using The Five Pillars of Success will give you the support to see your Vision through to completion.

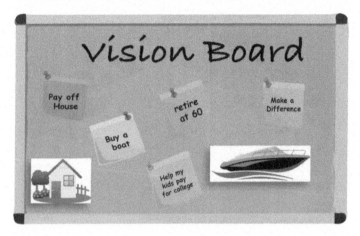

TAKE ACTION

Using your rePURPOSED Statement from lesson one and your Purpose created in lesson three, create your Vision. Your Vision is the image that you see when you think of what accomplishing your Purpose looks like. What would you like to achieve? This can be something you will accomplish within the next month or in a couple of years, or a success you will enjoy throughout the rest of your life.

Now, with that Vision, create a Vision Board.

A Vision Board can include any number of items that help remind you of your vision and encourage you to stay focused. Every person's Vision Board will look different. Make it your own. Do what inspires you.

Don't forget to include your WHY! You're why the motivation that will keep your commitment strong is.

Visit rePURPOSEDMIND.com for Vision Board ideas and resources. Following are a few Vision Board ideas:

• Pictures that represent your Vision, cut out of magazines and stuck to a poster board.

• An organized list of written actions that need to be taken to achieve the final Vision.

• An illustrated video with a voice-over and images describing the Vision.

• A picture in the center of a poster board that shows the final Vision surrounded by quotes to inspire, actions to take, dates to meet, and other photos that will inspire you to achieve that Vision.

A Vision Board needs to be something you physically see often. Print it, hang it up, put it somewhere that you regularly pass by, and where others will see it as well. When they see it, you can say, "This is my someday soon Vision. This is what I'm working toward."

It could have pictures of a beach, a restored vehicle, your company's stock listed in the S&P 500, or land with a cabin on it. Whatever that Vision is, create what works with *your* mind.

As you begin creating your personal Vision Board, you will likely experience doubts about being able to achieve your vision. You may see obstacles everywhere. How do you stay focused on your purpose when you have doubts? Remember the Five Rules of Purpose.

- Have fun
- Stay positive
- Embrace change and failure
- Make others look good
- Listen and be present

Let go of the things that limit you and replace them with things that you can take hold of. Things that will move you forward toward your Vision.

CREATE AN ABUNDANCE MINDSET

In 2020, during the COVID-19 pandemic, people panicked. They ran to the stores purchasing everything they could. Fear of running out of basic necessities overcame their awareness and concern for their communities. Shelves were wiped clean of disinfectant, hand sanitizer, canned goods, sugar, flour, and of course, toilet paper. People had responded with a scarcity mindset.

COVID-19 illuminated the impact on communities when a scarcity mindset invades an entire society. People hold tight to all they own waiting for scarcity to end. While the very existence of this scarcity is, ironically, a result of their mindset.

Thankfully, not all citizens approached the pandemic with a scarcity mindset. Some people handed out toilet paper to perfect strangers in parking lots. Despite economic uncertainty, others supported hard-hit local restaurants by increasing their patronage and picking up orders to go. People began offering to shop for older, higher-risk members of society. And businesses turned their resources and operations toward the production of much needed medical supplies. These people were responding with an abundance mindset.

A scene from *Doctor Who* illustrates this principle well. The scene opens with a boy and a man in a minefield, both clearly panicked. The man takes a step toward the boy and suddenly a hand from the ground grabs his ankle and he quickly disappears through the earth.

Terrified, the boy finds himself alone. He looks across the field, seeing hundreds of hands with eyes, looking up at him, waiting for him to step within their reach. Then he hears a voice. It's The Doctor's voice. He tells the boy he is there to help.

The boy asks, "Am I going to die?"

Doctor Who responds, "Your chances of living are 1000 to 1. Focus on the one. Believe you can live!"

When everything seems to be falling apart and a situation feels bleak with no end in sight, an abundance mindset allows you to focus on success, regardless of how small it may seem.

An abundance mindset is about *perspective*. Even during the worst of times, if you have an abundance mindset, you are able to give to others. When you have the perspective of abundance, anything is possible. In this mindset, you view failure as an opportunity for growth. You view obstacles as stepping stones. Nothing can stop you because anything that gets in your way is rePURPOSED to be a beneficial part of the process.

In the New Testament, Jesus Christ teaches this same principle: it's not about doing, it's about becoming. The Law of Moses was established on patterns of doing. However, Christ taught that the purpose of this law was not about what you do, but about who you become as a result of your actions. If someone slaps you on the cheek, give them your other cheek. If someone forces you to walk a mile with them, walk two miles. This is an abundance mindset. It's not so much about the actions you take, but about who you are and what you believe is possible.

You may find, however, that an abundance mindset does not come naturally to you. Your brain has been programmed for years with a scarcity mindset. So, how do you create an abundance mindset?

In his book, *The Miracle Morning*, Hal Elrod introduces the concept of "The Five Minute Rule." This rule says that it's ok to be frustrated, angry, or upset when things go wrong, but only for five minutes. When the five minutes are over you say three powerful words, "Can't change it." Hal explains that saying those three words reminds you that there is "no value in dwelling on something that is out of our control."

Focusing on what you want more of moves you past what you can't change to a state of abundance. Once you accept that you can't change what has happened in the past, it gives you the power to rePURPOSE your Mind to control how you respond to events in your life.

Be aware of *stop words*: "Can't, don't, won't, etc." When you use these words while communicating with yourself and others, your brain automatically focuses on the very things you are trying to avoid.

Many times, when visiting the pool, I've seen someone running and heard the familiar whistle and yell, "Don't run!" When you see someone running at the pool and yell, "Don't run!" they hear "run!" However, if you yell, "walk!" they know to walk.

Instead, use *go words*: "will, can, able, etc." Rather than saying, "I'm not healthy" say, "I am healthy because I drink enough water every day." Instead of setting a goal to "stop wasting time," set a goal to "achieve one extra task every day."

Words have so much POWER! When you shift your internal and external language, you can feel the positive reprogramming of your *go words*. They are powerful! The words you use have the power to rePURPOSE your Mind.

Still not sure your words are powerful? I have a client who felt that way. He struggled because every time he saw a beautiful woman, he found himself undressing her in his mind. He desperately tried to break this habit. The more he tried to stop, the more his mind focused on these beautiful women. I must add, he is a happily married man, so this habit *really* bothered him.

I offered my client a strategy. Instead of trying to deny a woman's beauty, why not accept it, acknowledge it and then immediately dismiss it. This method of mental redirection empowered him to rePURPOSE his Mind. Instead of focusing on stopping himself from mentally undressing beautiful women, he focused on accepting their beauty, and then quickly moving on.

After practicing this for a week, my client returned very excited. It changed everything. When he saw a beautiful woman, instead of trying not to notice her, he acknowledged her beauty and said to himself, "Bless you for this moment." And then he moved on. His mind no longer tried to take the time to undress women. Instead, he just appreciated the moment that their beauty gave him.

You probably know the story of David and Goliath from the Old Testament. There's a great lesson to be learned from David. After he slew Goliath, he was made king. One day while walking along his rooftop, he saw Bathsheba bathing, he was not wrong for seeing her. He was wrong for looking at her a second time. This was David's undoing.

When my client focused on trying *not* to undress beautiful women in his mind, he had, in effect, continued to look a second time. By changing his internal language, and acknowledging beautiful women, he was able to accept their beauty, dismiss it, and move on.

As illustrated in my client's experience, when you focus on what you *can't* do, what you *won't* do, or what you *don't* want to do, all of your attention and energy is directed to the very thing you are trying to avoid. You need to focus on what you *can* do, what you *want* to do, and what you are *capable* of doing. If you want to lose weight, avoid "negative" goals like "stop eating sugar" or "cut out all baked goods." When you create these goals, your brain immediately focuses on the sugar you *can't* have. Instead, set goals like, "eat more vegetables" or "exercise every morning." When you focus your efforts on *being* healthy, your brain will direct focus and energy into being healthy.

As you practice, you may begin to notice that everyone around you focuses on "can't." You may begin to identify those who have a scarcity mindset and those who have an abundance mindset. Your desire to be around those who speak abundantly will increase. You may also notice you are not as comfortable around those who have a scarcity mindset.

As you achieve more of an abundance mindset, your positive outlook may also affect the perception of those around you. The more you verbalize your abundance mindset, the more those around you respond. Your community may either choose not to be around you — because they don't want to handle that much positivity — or they'll want to be around you more because they *need* more abundance in their lives.

As you begin to see the world through an abundance mindset, those who are also looking for greater abundance will be drawn to you. As you learn to approach every roadblock and situation with what you CAN do, you will begin to see the opportunities open in your life. You will begin to notice the good, even in difficult times, and the opportunities others simply cannot see.

Only you are responsible for your own mindset. You are in control of your life and how you react to the events that unfold around you. When challenges arise greet them openly; *believe* in endless possibilities. This is the power of positivity.

LESSON

An abundance mindset is not so much about THINGS as it is about your perspective, but when you focus on what you *can't* do, what you *won't* do, or what you *don't* want to do, all of your attention and energy is directed to the very thing you are trying to avoid. When you have a perspective of abundance in your life anything is possible. You view failure as an opportunity for growth. You view obstacles as stepping stones. Nothing will stop you because anything that gets in your way is simply a part of the process to achieving your dream.

Where did that idiot learn how to drive!

I'm glad I have time to enjoy the scenery on my drive.

TAKE ACTION

It is easy to say nice things to other people. However, saying nice things to yourself is not always that easy. To have an Abundance Mindset, you need to transition your thinking to include saying nice things to yourself.

Make a list of those things that stand in your way. Think of things that you say to yourself that keep you from being able to achieve your Vision. Take those statements and rewrite them using an Abundance Mindset.

Here are some examples of what my clients originally said, and how they transitioned their thinking:

"I'm too old to change jobs."

"My age has given me years of experience to be the best person for this job."

"I don't like how I look in the mirror."

"This is my before picture. I can't wait to take my after picture."

"I don't make enough money."

"I'm looking forward to making more money so I can do more things with it."

"The people around me don't support me."

"I get to show people how truly amazing I am during their doubts."

"I don't trust any politicians."

"I'm grateful that I have the opportunity to make my voice heard by voting."

"I'm not a good parent."

"I am committed to being the best possible parent I can be and give myself a little bit of grace."

"I'm disorganized."

"My organization makes sense to me and keeps me focused."

Now it's your turn. Applying an Abundance Mindset, rewrite negative statements that you say to yourself.

1. _____

2. _____

3. _____

4. _____

5. _____

6. _____

Now that you have practiced turning your thoughts into thoughts of abundance, create a 90-day Abundance Mindset Action Plan (A MAP) for improving your mindset to one of Abundance. Review your A MAP at the end of each day. Celebrate every success, no matter how small. Ask yourself, "What did I do well?" Then evaluate how you can improve tomorrow. What action are you going to take to ensure your success? Your action plan can include ideas such as:

• Every time I think something negative, I will rePURPOSE that negative thought into one of abundance and text it to my friend.

• Each time I focus on something I don't like about myself; I will envision how I can change that to be something I'll love.

• When I find myself frustrated with another person, I will make it a point to say something positive about that person out loud.

Repurposing your Mind to an Abundance Mindset takes time and practice, especially when you have been programmed to think with a scarcity mindset. On rePURPOSEDMIND.com you can find some "force positive exercises." These exercises will help you practice rePURPOSING your Mind to see every situation with a positive perspective. You will find as you work on creating an Abundance Mindset putting it into practice becomes easier and easier as time goes on. With consistent practice, it will become a habit.

MOVE OUT OF JUDGMENT
AND INTO CURIOSITY

From a very early age, you were taught to approach situations with judgment. There are wrong and right answers to everything, especially in school. "Constructive criticism" is often an accepted way to say, "It's ok to judge you because it helps you." Throughout your life, it became natural to apply this thinking to every relationship, and you live in a natural state of judgment and criticism toward others and yourself. When you live in judgment, you approach others in order to convince them to agree with your way of thinking. Living in judgment constricts life's possibilities, limiting all your interactions, dreams and goals. This is a scarcity mindset.

When you approach people and ideas with curiosity, rather than judgment, you are able to appreciate anything that comes as a result. You are open to their ideas and create space for them to show up as they are and share what they believe in. You respect and appreciate why they think the way they do and accept that they find value in their own unique beliefs. Approaching life with curiosity means you allow people to be who they are, and in turn, you also allow yourself to show up as you are. Stay out of judgement, stay in curiosity.

There's an old story about a man who took his donkey to market carrying two sacks of wheat. On the way to the market he became tired, tied up his donkey and laid down to nap. When he awoke, he found his donkey was gone.

As he began to search for his donkey, he came upon a young boy and asked, "Have you seen my donkey?"

The boy replied, "Was he blind in his left eye, lame in his right foot and carrying wheat?"

Excited, the man said, "Yes, that's my donkey! Where have you seen him?"

The boy replied, "I have not seen the donkey."

Furious that the boy was clearly being lied to, he took the boy to the village magistrate to be punished. After hearing the story the magistrate asked the boy, "If you did not see the donkey, how did you know he was blind, lame and carrying wheat?"

The observant boy explained, "Only the grass on the right side of the road had been eaten, so I knew he could not see out his left eye. I noticed the left and right side of his tracks were different so I knew he was lame, and I saw grains of wheat all along the path."

As you read this story, what did you think? Did you also think the boy was lying? Or did you feel *curious*, wondering how the boy knew each unique detail if he had not seen the donkey?

Clearly, the man approached the boy with an attitude of judgment. Had he approached the boy with curiosity he would have simply asked, "If you did not see my donkey, how did you know my donkey was lame, blind in the left eye and carrying wheat?"

Approaching life with curiosity opens your mind to so many possibilities. Approaching others, including yourself, from a perspective of curiosity instead of judgment shows respect, care, concern and even love.

Often, acceptable judgment is branded as "constructive criticism." The thing is, criticism is *not* constructive. Criticism is telling someone they are wrong; it focuses on faults and mistakes of the past. A critical frame of mind is quite the opposite of constructive. When someone offers you "constructive criticism" it's like they are saying, "I'm hurting you because it makes you better."

What if, instead, they loved you and supported you because it made you better? What would it feel like to surround yourself with people who gave you "constructive support," focusing on how you could improve, instead of what you did wrong? "Constructive support" looks forward to the future. Support, unlike criticism, inspires you to achieve more and changes the focus from negative to positive.

Now, what if you were willing to do this for *yourself*? How might you step out of judgment and into curiosity? How could you offer yourself support instead of criticism?

It might look something like this: when you find yourself avoiding a task, instead of criticizing yourself for your lack of accomplishment ask yourself, "Is this actually something I would like to address right now?" If not, allow yourself to let go of that task. Accept yourself for who you are and what you are willing to do *in that exact moment*. Utilize those who support you to find an avenue for that task's completion.

Remember, if you aren't invested in a task, there's a likely chance you won't give it your all. It's time to accept that and move on to something you are willing to invest in. Understand that you are not letting yourself off-the-hook for not completing the task. You are simply giving yourself some grace to focus on tasks and actions you know you will take. Instead of being critical of yourself and getting bogged down by a to-do list you know you won't accomplish, allow yourself to put greater effort toward the things you know you will get done.

Look at what you CAN do, and what you WANT to do. From there the path forward will begin to open up.

The theologian Henri Nouwen is a great renowned spiritualist. He has written over 50 theological books since 1969 including *Life of the Beloved*, *The Return of the Prodigal Son*, and *The Inner Voice*. He once said,

"Often I have asked myself, what would it be like if I no longer had any desire to judge another? Or be controlled by the judgment of others? I would walk the earth as a very light person indeed."

Can you allow yourself to feel that lightness? What would it feel like to reserve judgement, and assign no weight to others' opinions of you? That is what it feels like to live curiously. When you approach life and your path to success with an attitude of curiosity, you open yourself up to all the possibilities you can imagine.

LESSON

Accept yourself for who you are and what you are willing to do *right now*. When you approach life and your path to success with an attitude of curiosity you open yourself to all the possibilities you can imagine.

TAKE ACTION

Create a list of tasks for tomorrow. Separate your list into "Will Do" and "Might Do."

Analyze your list of "Might Do." Reviewing each item, identify if they need to get done for you to move forward on your path to success. If the item does not need to get done, ask yourself if you will ever do this task. Be honest with yourself. If it doesn't need to get done and you know you won't do it, cross it off your list and move on to the next item.

With any of the remaining items on your list, ask yourself why it is not on your "will do" list. Consider your capability and capacity for each item. Perhaps it's because you just don't have time for that task tomorrow. If that's the case, move it to the next day or the next week. If it's because you simply dread doing the task, maybe you can hire someone to do the task for you. Ask how you can get constructive support to accomplish the task. Whatever it is, find a way to yes to accomplishing that task.

Once you have done this for tomorrow's tasks, do this for your tasks for the next week.

BE INTENTIONAL ABOUT
WHAT YOU SAY

Words are powerful. What we say to ourselves, what we say to others, and what others say to us can affect who we become, how we view ourselves, and how we interact with the world.

Personally, I know this to be true. Throughout my life, people have sometimes been frustrated with me for how slowly I completed work. However, those same people have also loved the results of my work. I remember the precise moment I was programmed to work slow and work well.

During a parent teacher conference when I was five years old, I was given a box of broken crayons and a picture to color while my teacher met with my parents. She told my parents, "Joshua is so slow. Everything he does is slow, but he does it really well. I love that about him, but it's frustrating how slow he works."

I remember thinking, "Somebody loves how well I work, even though I'm really slow. So, I'm going to be slow at everything because somebody will love it."

I was coloring a tree. I had chosen a few different shades of brown and green because I wanted the colors to come out like I imagined them. As I was layering these greens and browns on the tree, my teacher came over and said, "Have you been working on that one tree this whole time?" She was clearly trying to make a point to my parents.

I said, "Yes."

Then I looked at all the other papers she had given me to work on, and I realized they were assignments I should have finished during class time. She was giving me an opportunity to catch up, but instead of catching up, I focused on one thing. I did it very slowly, but very well.

The moment I remember most vividly are the words she spoke next, "I love how you put so many greens in the treetop and blended the browns of the trunk. It looks a lot like a real tree."

I was validated once again, "Be slow Joshua, because there will always be someone who appreciates the time you took to do it well."

Then she held up those other papers and said to my parents, "See."

I realized what was going on, but in that moment her words programmed me. I made a choice, at five years old, based on my teacher's words, to work slow and work well.

I share this story to illustrate that the words you speak to yourself have the same power that my teacher's words had with me in that moment. The words you choose will not only impact you, but those surrounding you.

The words you speak, think and share, program and shape you. Recently, I had a client say, "Look at me, just being a giver-upper." She was just joking, but the problem with self-degrading jokes is, *you are who you say you are*. If you choose to put those words out into the universe then those words are who you will become.

You may even do this with your loved ones. The words you jokingly speak to a friend or your kids, might very well program who they become.

I remember moments like that from my life. Words my parents said, and didn't mean. Phrases my teachers spouted, and quickly took back. Comments my friends made, and then laughed off. In those moments my community wanted to motivate me, but they didn't. It became programming that affected my whole life.

Those were the moments when I said, "Oh, that's who I am!"

If you were to pause and replay what you've said to your loved ones in moments like these, and then see a preview of how your words would affect their life long term, you would probably go, "Hold on! Don't take it the wrong way. Only apply it to this moment, this is not something you should apply to your whole life." What you say to others, even when you are joking, helps program who they become.

A client once chose to describe her organization style as "organized chaos." Why do you suppose she chose to add the word "chaos?" Well, she chose "chaos" because she thought I would judge her style and deem her unorganized.

But it doesn't matter what I think!

Her system worked, just the way she needed it to. By calling it "organized chaos" she programmed herself to believe that she was not actually organized, even though her system was in fact, perfect for her.

Sometimes you water down how you present yourself to others so they will reserve judgment. When you do this, you look through their filter and unintentionally program yourself to believe the words you spoke to them. Instead, choose to speak the words that truly represent you.

Many motivational speakers today teach about the power of words. One good example is the well-known coach Tony Robbins. He began his career as a motivational speaker, teaching people how to improve their lives through self-help and positive thinking. He wrote many books including: *Unlimited Power*, *Awaken the Giant Within*, *Giant Steps* and *Money: Master the Game*. When talking about achieving success he said, "The only way to achieve success is by believing you can achieve your goals, no matter what. The story you tell yourself has the power to transform your life or destroy it. When you change your story, you can change your life."

When things are difficult, what is your internal dialog? What do you tell yourself? Do you believe you can do hard things or do you put yourself down when challenges arise? Do you back up a belief that you are capable with your internal AND external words?

To create change during difficult times you need to rePURPOSE your Mind to the possibilities. Possibilities are limited only by your own beliefs. When you change your beliefs, your newfound language begins to write a brand-new existence for you to live in.

So what does that mean? The words you say out loud change. The words you say to others change. The dialog you have with yourself shifts as well. When that happens, your environment changes. You build a new world for yourself to live in.

You build it by believing you can be who you want to be, and then, internally and externally, speaking that truth into existence.

LESSON

Words are powerful. The words you say program you to who you will become. Be intentional about what you say about yourself both internally and externally. Be aware of who you think you are, because those thoughts program who you become. Be careful about what you say to others, your words help program them as well.

TAKE ACTION

Change Yourself

Answer these questions:

When things are difficult, what is your internal dialog? What do you tell yourself?

_____

_____

_____

_____

Do you believe you can do hard things or do you put yourself down when challenges arise?

YES / NO

Do you back up a belief that you are capable with your internal AND external words?

YES / NO

If you realize that you program yourself with negative words make a plan to change your internal dialog. You practiced this in the lesson "Creating an Abundance Mindset" with statements that keep you from reaching your Vision. Think about other statements you may use throughout your day and rePURPOSE your Mind with positive statements that will block the negative statements you say to yourself. For this exercise it is best to grab a notebook. Fold the sheet in half so you have two columns. On the outside column, write all the negative things you say to yourself throughout the day. Now on the inside column write a true positive statement that is opposite of each of your negative things.

Once you have all your positive thoughts written, tear out the half of the page that has your negative thoughts. Burn it, shred it, destroy it somehow and then throw it away.

Once you have your list of positive thoughts, read it every morning for the next three weeks.

CHANGE HOW YOU PROGRAM OTHERS

Think of how you talk to your family or friends. What words could you use in your communication with them that would help shape them into a more positive version of themselves?

Take those words, write them down with your other positive thoughts, and review them every morning for the next three weeks as well. This will help you remember who you want to be. It will also help you remember how you wish to speak with your friends and family. These words will recreate the world you live in.

YOU DON'T KNOW WHAT YOU DON'T KNOW

As you move forward on your journey to success, there will inevitably be things you don't know. You may be tempted to plan, and plan, and plan some more, in order to avoid these moments of not knowing. If you focus too much on the planning, you'll lead yourself into a trap where the planning stops you from doing. You won't know all the steps needed to reach your destination, nor will you be able to predict the various challenges that will arise along the way – and rest assured, unexpected challenges *will* arise. You cannot plan enough to avoid every problem. You simply don't know what you don't know.

That's okay.

Having an abundance mindset motivates you to begin even when you don't know everything. It isn't necessary to outline every step of the process. Just get going. In the next chapter, I'll share with you just how important small steps are to completing your journey.

The Author Michael A. Singer writes about using the energy inside you to focus your pathway toward what really matters to you. In his book, *The Untethered Soul*, he says, "People tend to burden themselves with so many choices. But, in the end, you can throw it all away and just make one basic, underlying decision: Do you want to be happy, or do you not want to be happy? It's really that simple. Once you make that choice, your path through life becomes totally clear."

Instead of allowing yourself to become overwhelmed with all the choices that you need to make to move along your path focus on this decision - you choose to be happy. As you focus on choosing happiness, the path forward will begin to open up even more. The unknowns will present themselves, and you will learn and grow with each new step. You will gain an increasingly clearer picture of the specific milestones you need to reach in order to understand your passion to achieve your purpose.

Stay flexible.

Let's say you plan to increase sales by a million dollars in two years. As time passes, you discover you are required by law to pay for insurance for your employees, something you did not know when you created your original plan.

Here you are, you have discovered something you did not know when you began. However, because you rePURPOSED your Mind with an abundance mindset, this surprise does not alarm you or stop you from moving forward. You can simply make it work. Sure, it cuts into your current growth projections. That's okay!

Remember the Rules of Purpose? You embrace the change and make the necessary adjustments in your budget and projections.

Does this mean you will have to adjust your final goal or timeline? Maybe. However, this new information also provides an opportunity for you to review your current progress and see if there is something you can add to your plan to keep you on track to meet your original goal.

Learning new information about running a business or reaching your desired goal is not a problem if you don't view it as one. It's an opportunity to re-evaluate, to step on top of that roadblock and get a better view of your situation. It's an opportunity to find a new way to expand your business or achieve your goal.

During the COVID-19 pandemic, most businesses saw a decrease in sales. Originally, no one knew this virus would force businesses to shut their doors. Sadly, some businesses shut their doors and never re-opened. Some were secure enough to survive. However, many businesses saw an opportunity and were flexible in their business structure and plan. They looked at the services they provided and the needs of their community and adjusted their model to address the present need. As a result, they didn't simply survive, they thrived.

A produce company in Spokane, Washington is a great example of this flexibility. Prior to COVID-19, they sold produce to local restaurants and when the restaurants closed, as a result of the governor's orders, they lost 70% of their business. They knew once the ban was lifted most of their business would return. They could have simply hunkered down and waited, but the owner saw a need and decided to sell his produce to the public directly.

Their business thrived under this new business model. They had so many sales, they were able to continue to support their current employees, and expand to hire family members who lost their jobs during the crisis. Selling to the public became so successful that they plan to make this a permanent part of their business model, even after the pandemic is over.

This company not only survived the pandemic, but through an abundance mindset, they saw an opportunity and created a new and lasting business success.

Remember to maintain your abundance mindset. It is during moments of adversity when you find success after you have learned to rePURPOSE your Mind. Start from where you are. Adjust your goals as you gain new insight. Then, with an abundance mindset, you will be able to triumph over any unknown challenges.

LESSON

Don't feel like you have to know every step of the process before you begin. As you move along, what you don't know will become apparent. This will give you an opportunity to re-evaluate your process. Adjust your goals as you gain new insight then move forward toward success!

TAKE ACTION

Create a 5-year action plan.

Where will you be with your Vision five years from now?

_____

_____

_____

Where do you need to be in three years to reach your five-year mark?

_____

_____

_____

Where do you need to be in one year to reach your three-year mark?

_____

_____

_____

Where do you need to be in three months to reach your one-year mark?

_____

_____

_____

Now create a list of actions you need to take in the next three months to reach that three-month mark.

_____

_____

_____

_____

_____

_____

_____

_____

Now act! Prioritize your list and get moving.

After three months, evaluate your progress and make adjustments if needed. Then create a new list of actions you need to take for the next three months to reach your one-year mark. Continue this process every three months.

GET UP AND GET MOVING

You may feel so far removed from fulfilling your Vision that it feels pointless to take a step toward it. It is critical for you to focus on success instead of letting the perceived distance between where you are now and where you want to be derail you from your envisioned path.

The key is to get up and get moving…

Take a step, no matter how small.

Even if the only action you feel capable of taking seems insignificant or pointless, do it anyway.

You might not have the strength to make it to the gym, but can you do one pushup?

Do it. Then add just one more each day.

You may feel too overwhelmed to spearhead that social media ad campaign you've been dreaming up. Are you able to run your ideas by someone who can provide valuable feedback or other resources?

Do it. Ask them to show you how.

If you don't know anyone who can help you with your current problem, can you go to an event where you might meet that person?

Do it. You might meet that person and build a lasting relationship.

Perhaps the most you can muster is forming the first phase of a plan to take action in the future.

Great. Do it. Then start on phase two.

No matter how tiny, actions generate results. You may be surprised by how much better you feel after taking a seemingly insignificant step. After all, one step leads to the next step, and the next, and so on. Before you know it, you'll look back at the progress you've made, and you'll be AMAZED.

Sometimes when we see a list of tasks that need to be done, we freeze. We think we can't possibly complete **everything** that needs to be done, so we don't do **anything**. In *Algorithms to Live By*, Brian Christian and Tom Griffiths explain how to use a "to do list algorithm" to help you get unstuck with your list of tasks. They describe three different algorithms to tackle a list.

1.   *Earliest Due Date*--Sort your tasks in order of due date and then start with the first task that is due. This will allow you to focus on getting the most urgent tasks done first.

2.   *Moore's Algorithm*--If you know it's not possible to complete all the tasks by their due date, skip the task that will take the longest. This will allow you to complete as many tasks as possible on time.

3.   *Shortest Processing Time*--Sort your tasks in order of smallest to largest. This works really well to help you when you feel overwhelmed. Once you are able to knock out several small tasks, you will begin to feel capable of tackling the bigger ones.

The authors do warn that with whichever algorithm you choose, you should beware of spending time doing unnecessary tasks in favor of tasks that are essential.

In the mid-twentieth century, Japanese business leaders were intrigued by the potential power of making small, incremental changes in pursuit of a larger goal. They invented a word for the concept: *Kaizen*. To this day, it remains a popular method for helping businesses thrive. That's because it works, both in business and personal success.

You may have a long way to go, but you aren't the first person to start from zero. Even billionaires like Bill Gates, Oprah Winfrey, and Elon Musk started with nothing. Focus on your destination and your vision instead of fixating on the distance to get there. If you dwell on everything that needs to be done, you will generate more resistance.

Instead, ask yourself what can be done *right now* – whether it's jotting down a few notes about a potential new product or service, searching the internet for someone who can design your new website, taking a shot at meeting a potential life partner, or simply drawing up a plan to take action in the future. Focus on your destination and your vision. Put one foot in front of the other and take the first step. Let your sense of accomplishment feed your soul as you begin to feel just a little less overwhelmed, and a little more inspired and hopeful.

Reap the benefits of your actions. Get up, and get moving.

LESSON

It is critical that you keep yourself from getting derailed by the seeming distance between where you are now and where you want to be. The key is to get up and get moving. With your focus on your destination, take a step, no matter how small.

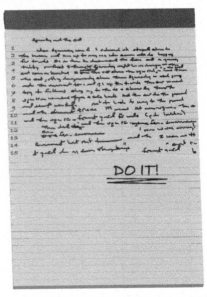

TAKE ACTION

Think about where you will be exactly one year from now? Make a list of anything that comes to mind that you know will need to get done in order for you to reach that one-year destination.

It's ok that the list isn't complete. Just write down whatever is swimming in your mind that you will accomplish within the next year. Here is some space for you to make that list.

_____

_____

_____

_____

_____

Now pick ONE thing that you can do right now and DO IT!

You may look at your list and think to yourself, "I can't do any of these items right this very minute, because it's 11pm!" Ok, what CAN you do? Look at your list closer and choose one of those items that you can break into smaller pieces. For example, maybe you put on your list, call 10 people to tell them about my new product line or service. Although it may be 11pm and not the right time to start making phone calls, you CAN *make a list* of ten people that you will call and set an appointment in your day tomorrow to do it.

No matter how small, there is something you CAN do right now which will move you toward your Vision.

Once you have completed that item look at your list and choose the next item you can do RIGHT AWAY and do it! As you continue doing these actions, no matter how small they seem in the moment, you will begin to feel energized. The momentum will carry you to the next item and the next. Before you know it, you will look back and see all the progress you made and how much closer you are to your year goal.

All it takes is one small step, one willing action, to get you moving toward your Vision.

SUCCESS REQUIRES SURRENDER

As you begin your journey forward, you will likely discover you have limited experience accomplishing certain tasks. Your journey is new, you might not have the foundation, training, or past experiences to lean on. You may need to turn to other's knowledge and experiences as you learn how to accomplish the tasks ahead of you. You will eventually learn to do it "your way," as you apply your unique approach to the challenges you face. In order to allow yourself to turn to others, it takes surrender.

This surrender is well illustrated in the series *Outsourced*. Todd, the main character, is sent to India to train call-center employees who sell novelty items to Americans. He begins by leading the Indian employees with his American expectations.

In one scene Todd answers employee's questions about the products they are selling. One employee asks about A221, a burger brand. Unfamiliar with how sacred cows are in India, Todd describes how American's brand their cows with a hot iron to show ownership. Mortified, one employee asks, "Wouldn't the cows run away?" Todd nonchalantly responds, "Oh, no, we only brand baby cows." At this point, Asha, one of the employees, raises her hand and says, "Mr. Todd, you need to learn about India."

Todd resists changing his perspective. He is so uncomfortable with anything outside of his known world, all he can think about is how to get out of India.

Later on, at a restaurant Todd runs into another American businessman who gives him a solid piece of advice, "I remember feeling like you. I was resisting India. Once I gave in, I did much better."

With this advice in mind, Todd goes out for a walk, unaware that it is the Indian Holiday, Holi. Caught in the middle of town, Todd is unexpectedly covered in colored chalk. At first he tries to escape, but as he accepts the tradition he starts to have fun. Todd begins to *surrender*. It is then that he realizes he has been trying to run the call center like an American office, and it isn't working.

He returns to the office, and asks his employees, "What would make your workday more positive?"

He receives requests ranging from filling their workspaces with family pictures, to wearing traditional clothing instead of western clothing. Once Todd surrenders and opens himself up to a new culture, he is able to support the employees in a way that creates joy and success.

Like Todd, you may feel resistant to change or the unknown. You may allow your ego to convince you your way is superior, even though it does not produce favorable results. I'm sure you've heard, "The definition of insanity is doing the same thing over and over again, but expecting different results."

Sometimes, certain patterns or processes need to be changed in order to succeed. Turning to those who have practiced these processes can give you a new perspective.

David Martyn Lloyd-Jones, a physician and minister, preached at London's Westminster Chapel for 30 years. He was famous for spending months preaching from a single chapter of the Bible, all while masterfully holding his parishioners' attention. One evening at a train station, Lloyd-Jones sat on a bench reading his Bible. A man next to him read *The Times*. The man looked up from his newspaper; recognizing Lloyd-Jones he said, "You're such a learned authority on The Good Book! How I wish I could be like you!" Smiling, Lloyd-Jones glanced at the man and replied, "Then put down your newspaper, and pick up your Bible."

Just as becoming an expert on the Bible requires the study of it, learning how to accomplish new tasks on your path to success requires studying those who have succeeded before you, and surrendering to what works.

So how do you succeed? It takes surrender. How do you achieve your vision? It takes surrender. How do you find out if the principles in this book will help you create lasting change in your life? It takes surrender!

Now is the time. Surrender.

LESSON

Sometimes, you need to look to the knowledge and experience of others as you learn how to accomplish the task before you. You need to learn how to do it the way that works for others while you learn how to do it "your way."

TAKE ACTION

Make a list of people you know who have knowledge or experience that could potentially help you achieve your Vision. Think about friends, family, business acquaintances, or clients. It does not even have to be someone you know. You can learn many things online from people who would otherwise be unreachable. For example, if you are starting a business and you want to do it without going into debt, you could access the personal money-management expert Dave Ramsey's collection of books, events, and other resources.

Now look at the tasks you have listed for the next three months. Identify any tasks in which you need more knowledge and who on your list could help. Commit to contact that person and learn from their knowledge and experience.

Name   Experience

EMBRACE RESISTANCE

Resistance accompanies every great effort, and embracing resistance is the path to any great success. When challenges block your path, the *attitude* you approach them with will dramatically affect your ability to succeed. It is natural to struggle when challenges block your path. However, you will have greater success if you are able to view these challenges as **opportunities** for growth and change, rather than **problems** that halt your progression.

When you're navigating a new path toward success you will inevitably meet resistance. There's no avoiding it— growth and resistance go hand in hand.

So ask yourself, how do you respond when you meet resistance? Do you allow yourself to feel discouraged? Do you give these obstacles the power to define your capabilities? Do you turn back and choose the path of least resistance out of fear?

Now, if you turn around and choose the path of least resistance, where will it lead you? Do you see yourself reaching your purpose when you *resist your resistance*? No, you turn around and head back to the start. You move further away from your purpose, rather than closer to it.

Obstacles will arise when you take action toward positive change. These obstacles come because you want to be different than what you are. The trick is learning to use these roadblocks to your advantage. That is why you must learn to *embrace resistance.*

In his book, *Positive Intelligence*, Shirzad Chamine discusses how your Positive Intelligence score (PQ), or the "measure of your mental fitness" determines how much of your potential you actually achieve. As you identify and overcome your mental saboteurs, such as judging, avoiding, playing the victim, controlling, and trying to please others, you increase your PQ.

By embracing resistance with high positive intelligence, we are able to use that resistance to help us move forward. Chamine says to look at a challenge we face and ask the following question, "What do we need to do so that within three years we can say this current crisis was the best thing that could have happened to our company?"

When you embrace resistance, your perspective is the key. You focus, not on who you once were, but on who you want to become; not on where you are now, but where you want to go. You focus on your goal.

So, why is focus so important? Because it influences what you see.

For example, if you are focused on finding yellow cars, you suddenly begin to see them everywhere, as if the number of yellow cars suddenly doubled or tripled in an instant. Of course, this isn't the case. The number of yellow cars is the same, but your focus is different.

The same is true of obstacles and goals. When you focus on your problems, they are all you see. When you focus on competition, it is everywhere. On the other hand, if you focus on your objectives, you will see them happening in your life. If you look to improve yourself, you take the steps to make it happen.

Once you're focused on your goal, ask yourself how the current obstacles in your path can help you reach success. When you encounter a roadblock, it isn't necessary to spend endless time figuring out how to move it, go around it, or tunnel under it. Instead, stand on top of it so you can gain a better view of your destination. View your obstacle as an opportunity to take a break and figure out the best path forward.

The fable of the farmer and the donkey is instructive here. A farmer's donkey fell into a well. The donkey cried, but no matter how hard the farmer tried, he could not rescue the poor animal.

Finally, the farmer gave up, deciding the best thing to do was to fill the well with dirt, so no one could fall in again. When the donkey realized the farmer intended to bury him, he cried even harder. Then, something amazing happened. Each time the farmer threw dirt on the donkey, the donkey shook the dirt off and stomped around on it. Before long, the growing pile had lifted the donkey to the top off the well, and he was free!

Instead of curling into a ball and accepting his fate, the donkey refused to yield. Every time the farmer threw dirt on him, he used his setback as a stepping stone. He literally climbed on top of his roadblock and found a way to move toward a solution.

You are the only person in charge of your success. You have the power to use resistance as your stepping stone to get there. When life's experiences feel like dirt falling on you, don't curl up and accept your fate. Instead, shake it off your back. Focus on what you can do with this dirt, and how you can use it to your advantage on your path to a solution. *Embrace resistance to achieve success.*

LESSON

It is natural to struggle when a challenge blocks your path; however, you will have greater success if you view the challenge as an **opportunity** for growth and change instead of a **problem** which stops your progression. Perspective is the key.

TAKE ACTION

There's resistance. Time is often resistance; you want things done now. Money is often resistance; you don't have enough to do what you need. Your own inner dialogue sometimes speaks negative thoughts into your mind creating resistance. All of these things are present resistance. Look at these things as your future self. When your future self looks back at problems, it's easy to see the solutions.

Writing to your future self, complete the following:

My biggest problem I have right now is

_____

_____

_____

_____

Your future self thinks your present problems are small. You've already solved them and moved on. With this in mind, write back from your future self:

That problem was small. We already solved it by

_____

_____

_____

_____

FOCUS ON THE PROCESS

In certain moments you may feel stuck. In these times, your challenges may be so overwhelming that reaching your Vision feels hopeless. When you are feeling this way, you may also be tempted to "play the victim" and blame your circumstances and choices on other people or events. After all, if you are not responsible for getting yourself into your current situation, it only makes sense that you are not responsible for getting yourself out, right?

Wrong.

In order to start making progress toward your Vision, you must first take responsibility for your life, the choices you make, and the actions you take.

So how do you take responsibility? How do you carry the heavy and burdensome weight of your challenges on your back?

Focus on the process.

When you stop making excuses and blaming others you are able to *refocus*. You create space to ask yourself questions. What do you actually want? What is truly getting in your way? What can you do to overcome or reframe these obstacles? How can you move forward?

Focus on the process.

This is exactly what Navy SEAL, Marcus Luttrell, did after his team of four was ambushed by a much larger force of Taliban fighters in rural Afghanistan. His entire team was cut down. He was shot and alone in hostile territory. A nearby rocket even exploded and injured his leg. Despite his circumstances, he focused on the process. He trained his mind on the next step. He focused away from overwhelm and blame; and instead on the answer to one simple question "*what's next?*" He gave himself a mission: find water. Once he found water, he asked again, "what's next?" This focus started a chain reaction that ultimately enabled him to make it back home alive.

Like Marcus, you must stop fixating on your circumstances. Stop convincing yourself you are powerless. Refocus. Take ownership of your life. No complaining. No comparing. No looking for blame in others. Instead, commit to action, and ask yourself: "what's next?"

If you focus on the process, soon enough you're next, "what's next" will be your Vision coming to fruition.

LESSON

When you feel stuck, it can affect other people or events. In order to make progress toward your goals, you first have to take responsibility for your life, the choices you're making and the actions you're taking.

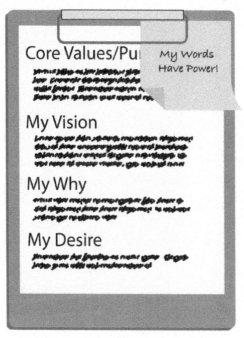

TAKE ACTION

In order to focus on the process, you need to know what it is. In the last two chapters you identified your five-year Vision plan and the tasks you need to take for the next three months. Now let's identify your process when things get overwhelming.

Marcus Luttrell made it through getting caught behind enemy lines because he had been trained again and again what to do in a life or death situation. He already knew the process and could recall it because he had practiced it.

So, when you hit roadblocks, when your Vision begins to feel too far for you to ever reach, when something gets in your way of moving forward, what will you do? What is your reACTION Plan?

Create a reACTION Plan now. Consider what you will do to keep moving forward when you feel like all is lost. List the steps you will take when everything seems to be falling apart. Be sure to consider everything you will need to be able to reset yourself on your path to your Vision. This will include some reflection and much action. Here are a few ideas I recommend you include in your reACTION Plan:

• Review your core values and your Purpose. Are your current actions staying true to your core values and Purpose? Is there anything you need to change to realign your actions?

• Review your Vision. Do you still believe in your final goal? Has anything changed?

• Review your "Why." Why are you pursuing this Vision? Has your "Why" changed?

• Review your Desire. Have you allowed someone else's filter to direct your actions away from your true focus?

- Reevaluate your 1-year, 3-year, 5-year goals. Are they valid? Are your actions still moving you toward those goals?

- Identify actions that need to be adjusted and who is responsible for making sure those actions are met.

- Answer the question: What's next?

Here is some space for you to create your plan. Remember to review it frequently and adjust it as necessary.

_____

_____

_____

_____

_____

_____

_____

_____

_____

_____

_____

_____

_____

Now you are ready to face those moments of uncertainty with a plan that will keep you moving forward toward your Vision.

STOP LYING TO YOURSELF

Yes you! Stop lying to yourself

When it comes to uncompleted tasks, everyone lies. Even you may convince yourself that something beyond your control is stopping you from accomplishing your tasks. You might make excuses and promise yourself, or your coach, that you'll complete the tasks at hand — next week. Sound familiar? Despite what you may think, cutting other commitments out of your schedule will not solve your problem.

The trick is honestly identifying WHY you aren't completing your tasks in the first place.

You lie to yourself and others for two reasons: one, because you don't want to do the work, or two, because your actions aren't being led by your passion.

Let's start with reason number one. Any vision or idea includes tasks that you don't want to complete. So, what do you do if you are simply avoiding the task because you don't want to do the work?

It starts with turning an idea into immediate action. Anytime you have an idea, act on it within 40 seconds. If you choose not to act immediately, you won't act at all.

Acting on your ideas can take many forms. Action might look like scheduling a phone call, or writing your idea down in a planner. Maybe it's even making the time to complete the task right then.

Everyone has a unique process and you need to trust and utilize the process that works best for you. It may be keeping a list in a notebook, or perhaps you use online tools, like Trello or Remind. You may even wish to hire someone to track your tasks for you. Whatever your process is, you do you!

Moving forward, examine every idea with the following questions in mind. Is this important enough to do right now? Is this important enough to take the time right now to schedule a future time to complete it? Is this important enough to pay someone else to do it right now? If the answer to all these questions is no, then decide if it really needs to be done or if it's just a nice idea.

If your idea *needs* to be acted upon, do it within 40 seconds.

If, on the other hand, you are avoiding acting on an idea because it is not true to your purpose, you need to reevaluate your Vision and desire. Is this really the direction you want to take? Is your Vision still clear and your desire still high? Is your idea based on someone else's filter?

If you're avoiding your tasks because you're unclear or uninspired by your Vision, you may feel like one of my clients did.

My client was discouraged, disheartened and quite frankly, ready to fire me. She said she wasn't getting anywhere, so she thought she needed a different coach.

So I responded, "Alright. Let's see where this fell apart. Which agreed upon monthly tasks did you complete?"

She thought about it and realized that she had not completed any of her tasks. Then she replied, "I'm the problem."

She recognized her own unwillingness to take immediate action toward her goal. So, she stepped back, reevaluated her Vision, and identified the actions she was WILLING to take in order to achieve her goals.

Sometimes you have to reevaluate your ideas. If you are not willing to complete the actions required to achieve your goal, then your idea does not match your passion. You need to discover what you are willing to do, and once you find clarity, move forward and do it. When your Purpose is clear, you are able to differentiate which ideas need to be acted upon, and which do not serve your larger Purpose and Vision.

So, be ready to act on your ideas in 40 seconds, or ask if your idea really needs to be completed to serve your Purpose. As you act upon and evaluate your ideas, you may even gain clarity about your Purpose or re-evaluate your Vision.

As you decide whether to act or move on, remember to be honest with yourself. You don't have the time to lie to yourself anymore.

LESSON

When it comes to completing a task, we all lie. We lie to ourselves and others because we either don't want to do the work, or our idea isn't true to our passion. Re-evaluate your Vision and honestly ask yourself "Is this truly who I want to become?" Whatever the answer, be honest with yourself and either take action or move on.

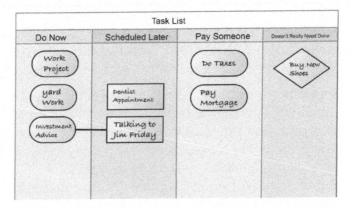

TAKE ACTION

Make a list of the tasks that you just can't seem to get to. You might even borrow from the list you made in Chapter 7.

1. _____

2. _____

3. _____

4. _____

5. _____

Ask the following questions about each task:

Is this important enough to do right now?

Is this important enough to take the time right now to schedule a future time to complete it?

Is this important enough to pay someone else to do it right now?

If the answer to all these questions is no, then ask:

Does this task really need to be done?

If the answer is yes to any of those questions, write something you can do right now to take action on that task.

1. _____

2. _____

3. _____

4. _____

5. _____

Your action can be scheduling a time to get it done and telling someone to keep you accountable. It can be setting up an ad or buying a bot right now to pay someone else to do the work. It can even be setting a timer and actually beginning to do the task.

Whatever the action is, do it NOW!

Follow this process for every task you continue to put off.

IDENTIFY YOUR TRIGGER

I want you to think for a moment about one of your bad habits. A behavior you're sure you could change — if you really wanted to. Perhaps you drink too much, binge on sweets, or spend endless hours scrolling through social media.

Alright, do you have it?

Now, think. What causes you to indulge in your bad habit? What triggers you? Really think about it. Is it stress or worry? Is it an argument with someone? Is it boredom?

Chances are, you'll be able to identify your trigger pretty quickly.

So, let's take this one step further. *What triggers you to **stop** believing you can achieve your Vision or become the person you want to be?*

Is it a comparison to someone else? A roadblock you can't find a way to climb on top of? Your mindset? The words of a well-intentioned loved one? Maybe you're not sure yet - so let's explore.

When you first discovered your Purpose you felt excited, like you could do anything! You created a plan, made goals, and began moving forward.

Then something happened.

An unexpected challenge appeared and you had no idea how to respond. You thought, "This isn't what I thought it would be."

Stop. Think about a moment when you suddenly felt like you could not keep going. What caused your hesitation? What made you react poorly to the situation you encountered?

Triggers distract you from your Purpose. They cause you to forget why you decided to take action toward your Purpose in the first place. You may need someone outside yourself, like a coach, who can help you identify your unique triggers. Once you identify your triggers you recognize them when they occur and can redirect them and rePURPOSE your Mind.

So what do you do once you know how to identify your triggers?

Look at it this way, have you ever had a muscle cramp? When your muscle cramps, your natural inclination is to pull the muscle tighter. But the way to relieve the cramp is to do the opposite, stretch the muscle out and go against the tightening of the muscle.

The same is true with triggers. You naturally respond in a certain way to your unique triggers. In order to become the person you want to be and to reach your Vision, you must identify the triggers that push you into a place where you cramp up. Instead of avoiding, make a new choice and to do the opposite, respond in a way that cares for you rather than hurts you further.

Once you identify your trigger, rePURPOSE your Mind by creating a positive response to that trigger. This new response will quickly become a habit as you continue to put this new reaction into practice.

For example, if stress triggers you to eat, choose to recognize your stress and go for a walk. If self-doubt triggers your work results to diminish, choose to recognize your self-doubt and text a friend something positive about your work day.

The way you respond to a trigger makes all the difference. Identify your trigger and accept it. Then choose a healthy way to rePURPOSE your Mind in that moment. This redirection will allow you to reach your Vision as the person you want to become.

LESSON

Triggers distract you from your Purpose. Identify your trigger and accept it. Then identify a healthy way to rePURPOSE your Mind in that moment. This redirection will lead you to who you want to become.

TAKE ACTION

The purpose of this action is to help you identify your triggers and rePURPOSE your Mind to respond to that trigger in a positive way.

First of all, what are your triggers? What happens in your life that stops you from moving forward to a goal or accomplishing a task? Think about a moment when you suddenly felt like you could not keep going or the goal wasn't worth achieving. What triggered your hesitation?

The answer may not come quickly to you. Allow yourself the time you need to reflect and properly identify what triggered you. Try to think about more than one instance in your life that you suddenly felt like not working toward something you wanted to do. Think about the events in your life, the feelings you felt. What turned your mind from thinking "I can do this," to thinking "maybe not."

Once you know it, write it down.

_____

_____

Now think about how you respond to that trigger. It may be a specific action you take, like binge eating, or it may be negative thoughts that invade your mind.

Once you know your trigger and how you respond, rePURPOSE your Mind by creating a positive response to that trigger. Think about how you currently respond and write down a positive response that will counteract it. For example, if your response to your trigger is to binge on junk food, your rePURPOSED response could be that you will go for a walk. If your response is to think negative thoughts, take those negative thoughts and rePURPOSE them to an Abundance Mindset. Write, "When [describe your trigger] I will [describe your new response]."

_____

_____

_____

Just knowing your trigger and creating a new response will not be enough. You need to focus on it every day. Reread the new response that you wrote above, *out loud* every day for at least three weeks. Reading it out loud will engage more of your senses, training your mind to know what to do when your trigger appears. If three weeks is not enough, keep reading it for as long as it takes until the new response becomes natural to you.

OWN YOUR SUCCESS

When you experience success and someone compliments you on a job well done what is your immediate reaction? Do you say, "Thanks, but I didn't really do that much. I just got lucky"? Do you pass all the credit to another by responding, "My friend did all the heavy lifting"? If your reaction is similar to the above examples, you might be self-sabotaging. By refusing to claim ownership, you remove your ability to own your success.

Why do you do this?

It might be because success scares you. When you accept and own your success, you claim responsibility for your future success. By deflecting responsibility and attributing the success to someone or something else, you avoid the continued responsibility of building upon your own original achievement.

When people deflect their success, they do it to relinquish the responsibility of future failures.

What if you accepted responsibility for your successes and then ended up failing? Does the thought of failure cause your heart to stop? Do you feel like quitting before you've even started if the possibility of failure exists?

Failure can be a hard pill to swallow, especially when you've worked hard to achieve something. It's much easier to accept failure when someone or something else has ownership over the failed project.

In the words of Robert T. Kiyosaki, founder of the Rich Dad Company, "Winners are not afraid of losing. But losers are. Failure is part of the process of success. People who avoid failure also avoid success."

Consider this, if your success is a result of luck, or another person's actions, then do your actions even matter? If this is the case, you have **no** control over your success, your destiny, or future progress. If you have no control, then you have no responsibility. Your actions do not matter, nor does your hard work. It's simply all a game of chance and you may, or may not, be the lucky winner.

What if you take responsibility for your success? What if every success is a result of one specific action? What if every action you take, every smile you share, every call you make, and every list you compile moves you closer to achieving your vision? And what if part of that success includes opportunities for failure?

Your view of success and failure is determined by your mindset. With an Abundance Mindset, even failure has a place in progress. With an Abundance Mindset you either land the deal or you learn from the rejection. With a rePURPOSED MIND, failure is a natural part of success. Failure occurs so you can see the correct path to take next time. Failure leads to success.

Thomas Edison understood this when he said, "I have not failed. I've just found 10,000 ways that won't work."

When you are tempted to pass your success on to others, step back and review the actions *you* took which resulted in success. Analyze every action. Think about every detail. When you reflect on your actions as potential causes of success, you will see how each action led to your ultimate achievement. Through reflection and awareness you can realize *your power* to succeed. In turn, you will be able to own your success.

So, by all means, when you succeed, take credit! Bask in the moment. Savor it. Own your success! As you do, your perspective of success will shift, and the vast possibilities before you will appear. You will come to see how owning your success and failure allows you to achieve, prosper, and win. As you take ownership of every action, every success, and every failure, you will rePURPOSE your Mind to gain control of your Vision. You will succeed, when you own your success.

LESSON

With a rePURPOSED MIND, failure is a natural part of success. As you take ownership of every action, every success, and every failure, you will rePURPOSE your Mind, understanding your passion and gaining control of your Vision. You will succeed.

TAKE ACTION

Have fun with this activity! I want you to make a list of your successes.

Think about times you won and identify how you contributed to that success. I don't want just your recent successes. Remind yourself of the things you accomplished even early in your life.

My Success

_____

_____

What/How I Contributed to That Success

_____

_____

My Success

_____

_____

What/How I Contributed to That Success

_____

_____

My Success

_____

_____

What/How I Contributed to That Success

_____

_____

My Success

_____

_____

What/How I Contributed to That Success

_____

_____

My Success

_____

_____

What/How I Contributed to That Success

_____

_____

Now I want you to think about times you "failed." I put "failed" in quotes because I truly believe with an Abundance Mindset, you never really fail; you either win or learn from every experience.

So think about these times that you "failed" and how that failure brought you closer to success. What did you learn from each failure or how did that failure lead you into a different direction toward a different success?

Time I "Failed"

_____

_____

What/How That "Failure" Brought Me Success

_____

_____

Time I "Failed"

_____

_____

What/How That "Failure" Brought Me Success

_____

_____

CHOOSE YOUR WINGMAN

Ask any successful person if they have a coach, a mentor, or a trainer and they will say "Yes!" They have someone who they confide in on a regular basis, someone who sets them straight, lines them up for success, and ensures they won't be derailed. Everyone needs someone to keep them accountable. Success is impossible without proper support.

This is what I call the wingman philosophy. In today's world, your wingman might help you win a big deal at work. They may do so by giving you courage, and supporting you through the sales process. They may help you stay focused when you find yourself faced with distractions.

The term "wingman" began as a military term and dates back as far as World War One.

In a fighter sequence, the wingman is positioned behind, and to the right of, the lead fighter's right wing. From this position the wingman watches the lead's back, and increases their awareness and firepower. This allows the lead to approach with more dynamic tactics and better focus. In the military, the wingman is the most trusted and essential role in the flight formation. The wingman always stays with the lead, despite the cost. The wingman must have the best set of eyes and be willing to put their ego aside, giving the glory to the lead.

The same is true for your wingman. Your wingman's responsibility is to watch your back, keep their eyes out for potential problems, support you, and increase your "firepower," to help you stay focused on your main goal. It is not about them, it's about you.

When you have a wingman you take bigger, bolder, sometimes even potentially more reckless leaps. You're always braver when someone else is by your side. So, when the choices you make depend on the type of wingman you have, it's important to *choose carefully*.

You want a wingman who will hold you to your Vision and values and lay down a firm line if they see you veering off track. They are not afraid to call you out when you play the victim or wallow in fear and doubt. You need a wingman you can go to on a regular basis to set you straight, and keep you from getting derailed. You are not looking for them to just be an agreeable friend or a pal.

A wingman usually serves one of three different roles: a partner, a mentor, or a coach.

A partner has a vested interest in your project. You both exert effort in a shared goal. A partner either strengthens you or weakens you. With a partner as your wingman, you are only as strong as your weakest link. This can also be a really beneficial relationship where both partners work equally as hard to support their mutual success.

A mentor is usually someone who has already walked the path you are currently on. They help you through the process of avoiding the mistakes they made. A mentor focuses purely on action and activity. They help you replicate their success. You may or may not follow the same mentor through your whole process.

A coach helps you with your mindset. You expect them to hold you accountable for the goals you collectively create. They assist you in both developing an action plan and following through with it. A coach helps you see challenges from a different perspective. They also give you increased firepower by helping you multiply successful actions. A coach helps you throughout your whole process so you can stay focused on your Vision.

It is possible to have more than one wingman. You may have a partner in your business, a mentor to help direct you through a certain task, and a coach who helps you stay focused on your ultimate Vision. Just make sure your wingman elevates and inspires you. Finding the right wingman can be one of the most powerful components of achieving your dreams. With an amazing wingman by your side, you will soar higher than you ever thought possible.

Now it's time for you to truly commit and rePURPOSE your Mind. Who do you know that can provide support as you follow the principles of this book? Who in your circle can be your wingman as you achieve your Vision?

Perhaps a coach gave you this book to read. They care about you and want you to understand the vocabulary of success; hire them! Maybe you found this book on your own and the message deeply resonates with you. Determine what kind of wingman will best support you at this point in your journey, and find someone to fill that role.

With the right wingman and a rePURPOSED MIND your success is closer than ever before.

LESSON

Finding the right wingman can be one of the most powerful keys to achieving your dreams. With the right wingman by your side, you will have greater success than you ever thought possible.

TAKE ACTION

List the people you know who may already be your wingman.

As you review this list, remember you want someone who:

- Supports you
- Keeps their eyes out for potential problems
- Helps you stay focused on your Vision
- Stays with you throughout the process
- Sees things you may not see
- Gives you the glory. This is not about them, it's about you
- Holds you to your Vision and core values

- Lays down a firm line to keep you on track of your Vision

- Calls you out when you play the victim or wallow in fear and doubt

- Sets you straight

- Keeps you from getting derailed

- Elevates and inspires you

- Understands the importance of an Abundance Mindset in achieving your goals

The person who meets the greatest number of qualities on the list is your strongest wingman. You may have more than one, and that's okay. Each wingman most likely supports you in a different way. Understanding where their strengths lie will help you know who to turn to when you need a wingman most.

I want to be your wingman. At rePURPOSED MIND, I provide coaching and consulting for people who are ready to take the next step to greater success. If you are still on the journey to rePURPOSING your Mind, I have additional resources available at rePURPOSEDMIND. com. Your success is important! Don't wait to get started on the next step, take action today to turn your Vision into success.

.GLOSSARY

Abundance Mindset: Viewing failure as an opportunity for growth and obstacles as stepping stones. A positive perspective that allows you to view anything as possible.

Abundance Mindset Action Plan (A MAP): 90 day plan you design to improve your mindset to one of Abundance.

Constructive Support: Focusing on the good of a situation to inspire you to achieve more and change the focus from negative to positive.

Core Value: The foundation of who you are. The qualities that define your passion and purpose.

Desire: The measure of how badly you want to pursue an idea.

Five Pillars of Success: Five steps to turn your ideas into successes.

Force Positive Exercises: Exercises that will help you practice seeing every situation with a positive perspective.

Go Words: Words that focus your mind toward the positive. i.e.: Will, can, able, etc.

Idea: The starting point for pursuing your success.

Motivation and Commitment: Why you want to achieve your vision and how strong your desire is to reach your success.

Purpose: The knowledge of how you will exemplify your core values. The path you will follow to reach your goals.

Reaction Plan: The plan you create that will help you stay focused on the process when you hit roadblocks.

Repurposed MIND: The ability to recognize failure is a natural part of success. The end result of shifting your mind to an Abundance Mindset.

Repurposed Statement: A statement that defines who you will be, what you will do, how you will achieve access and who you serve.

Repurposing your Mind: The action of following the exercises in this book to shift your mindset from one of scarcity to one of abundance.

Rules of Purpose: Five rules to help you stay focused on your purpose and not get distracted by the process.

Stop Words: Words that draw your attention to a negative focus. i.e.: Can't, don't, won't, etc.

Success: Achieving your vision. Success should also be celebrated as you overcome obstacles along your journey.

Trigger: The cause behind a negative response. Triggers distract you from your purpose.

Vision: The end goal of your journey - what do you expect to get out of your path to success.

Vision Board: A visual representation of what accomplishing your purpose looks like.

Willing Action: Purposeful movement toward your vision. What you are willing to do to make your success happen.

Wingman: A person, or people, you identify to help you stay focused on your mail goal.

Your "Why": The motivation that will keep your commitment strong. The reason behind your vision.

WORKS REFERENCED

Borden, Robert, creator. *Outsourced.* In Cahoots Productions, Universal Media Studios, and Open 4 Business Productions, 2010-2011.

Brown, Brené. *Dare to Lead.* Random House, 2018.

Chamine, Shirzad. *Positive Intelligence.* Greenleaf Book Group Press, 2012.

Christian, Brian, and Griffiths, Tom. *Algorithms to Live By.* Henry Holt and Company, LLC, 2016.

Elrod, Hal. *The Miracle Morning.* Hal Elrod, 2017.

Roth, Bernard. *The Achievement Habit.* HarperCollins, 2015.

Sinek, Simon. "How Great Leaders Inspire Action." *TEDxPuget Sound,* September 2009, www.ted.com/talks/simon_sinek_how_great_leaders_inspire_action

Singer, Michael A. *The Untethered Soul.* New Harbinger Publications and Noetic Books, 2007.

ACKNOWLEDGEMENTS

I want to thank Jennifer Vest; without you my words would not have become this book. Thank you to Annalise Combs for assisting with editing and to Taegan Williams for creating the chapter illustrations.

ABOUT THE AUTHOR

Joshua Dahlstrom has been coaching for over 13 years. As a success coach, he has helped hundreds of business men and women find their purpose and attain success. He has a proven track record of success in marketing, and has run a successful marketing business while coaching clients to rePURPOSED success.

Joshua has combined his skills in coaching with his sales and marketing experience to position companies and individuals for more growth opportunities. He has helped many companies gain more value through their purpose-directed functions to achieve their revenue growth goals. Through coaching, he has taught sales teams to adopt best practices for time management, prospecting, achieving client solutions, and methods to refine and grow sales pipelines.

His Vision is to change families, neighborhoods, communities, organizations and the world by helping them overcome obstacles that are keeping them from achieving their own success.

He loves practicing what he preaches and currently works with Intrinium, a fast-growing cyber security firm, where he coaches the sales and marketing teams to phenomenal success.

Joshua and his wife have four creative children who love art, music, and the outdoors. Visit him at JoshuaDahlstrom.com to stay in touch.